To Rosie

"I'd love to hear you"

Violently Tender
(Performance Poetry)

Abraham Gibson

Second Edition 2002
First published in Great Britain 2001
by Pen Press Publishers Ltd
39-41, North Road
Islington
London N7 9DP

ISBN 1 900796 64 3

Printed and bound in the UK by
Antony Rowe Ltd
Chippenham, Wilts

A catalogue record of this book is available
from the British Library

Dedicated to my dad, Desmond Gibson
(28 March 1935 – 29 March 2001)

'I'll see you when I'm looking at you!'

Acknowledgements

With special thanks to my brothers and sisters:
Robert Gibson – 'It's a giraffe, man.'
Jeff – 'The sky is open.'
Stafford – 'There's plenty of time.'
Tim, from Zimbabwe to Forest Gate,
you're always there.
Merline, your mind is brilliant, your heart is beautiful,
but your dresses are too short.
Twiz (Nadine), my sister, I miss you.

For all my nieces and nephews:
Ryan – thanks for meeting us anywhere.
Robert – smile, you know the ladies love it.
Ashley, Reece, Grant, Khai, Dayna –
thinking of you.
Stella, Amina, Jade, Naomi –
you are all so beautiful.
Little baby Paul – welcome.

The Brothaman collective – thanks for providing
support, encouragement and a stage.

To my drinking partners, Joel Mintus, Johnny Boy
Mendy and Kevin: 'Just one more, man.'

Harry, I hope your kindness and thoughtfulness is
apparent in these pages.

Naana – give it a shot

And thanks to:
Veronica Owens for the cover illustration.
Marc Maroney – 'salmon like'.
Delores Springer for her encouragement.
Janet Plummer for scaffolding conversations
'Eyes' Jimmy – you see everything, man.
Maz, wiselike.

Mum – 'maybe, might, should be, can'.
Zena Edwards, for the healing pool.
Victoria Mosley – thanks for believing in me.
Omi Shade – 'yellow till gold'.
Wayne Howlett and Pauline O'halloran –
you're in my heart.

Edna, for giving me books with such passion –
I read them likewise.
Laureen Hickey, my teacher, who has passed on –
I'm still listening for your lessons.
Linda Lloyd, for your editing – what grace.
Catrina Sherlock – for bringing the cover to life.

For my wife Paulette –
Shelter, food and you, and a beautiful garden.
Your love must be laced with rum; I haven't been
sober since we met.

And my children Bezaleel, Dalmar, Nathaniel.
Meet me anywhere ...

And God has more than enough love for all of us.
Thank God for that!

Contents

* Extracts from the stage play, *Evening for Blueness*, by Abraham Gibson

She Says, 'I Don't Love You, But You Can Kiss Me If You Want To.'

She says,
'I don't love you, but you can kiss me if you want to,
     on the understanding that
     I ... don't ... have to kiss you back!'

What's a man to do ... ?

I kissed her preciously, passionately
throughout the night
In the morning she began to cry

When I asked her why she was crying
she said,
       'because your kisses remind me
        of how I used to feel!'

       I asked if I could see her again one
       day.

She promptly said, 'No!'

I enquired as to the reasons why not.

She said,
       'I don't want to use up your kisses
       the way my kisses were ...!'

I told her that her kisses
were not used up, they are in her soul,
like butterflies making her heart ache.

She smiled and responded,

'If that were true,
                if ... that were true ...
        what would you do
                if I were to release them?'

I told her I'd light a candle, to see all their faces
and kiss them back.

She says,
'I don't love you, but you can kiss me if you want to!'

Nancy and Reva

NANCY: Well, I've lived on this estate
for 55 years now
and I'd like to be able to say
that nothing really surprises me
but surprise, surprise
(*with emphasis*) – it still does!

NANCY *starts to clean her window. The spotlight
follows her.*

The way that the bare trees
in the park
throughout the winter make me cry.
I know it's silly
but winter has a way of making you believe
there never was a summer
After a good cry I feel better:
at my age any little bit of moisture does
you good.

*She leans towards the audience, as if speaking in
confidence.*

Only the other day I was saying:
next summer, will I see those branches
blossom with leaves?
Don't get me wrong (*taking off her
glasses*), my eyes are still good
but the nights are so long
and the stairs to the ground floor
so eerie.
Before I face them I sit and wonder

if I'll be able to make the round trip.
God forbid me getting stranded at the bottom.

She sits down in a chair, addressing the audience again

When I was younger
all I ever really worried about
was my hair
and something nice to wear
but all this blackness of winter
and greyness in the mirror
is the closing of my yesterdays.

Sometimes I feel I hold onto them so

tightly,

I'm squeezing all the colour out of them.

The lifts work
when they want to
but like anything man-made,
when they go wrong
you're not surprised.
I never use the lifts,
not because I feel ...(*thinks of a word*)
claustrophobic –
and that's a hell of a word
I learnt to pronounce,
don't bloody like it –
no, not because I'm claustrophobic
but they smell so bad
and look so (*with emphasis*) dirty.

NANCY *gets up again and resumes cleaning the window.*

It's a real journey, them stairs,
you never know when the doors will open
and, if they open, who'll be waiting.
I know it's supposed to make the climb easier,
(*to audience*) but sharing a lift
with a young, drugged-up squatter
and his skinny flea-pit dog
can stretch a journey
beyond all reasoning.

And my coloured friend Reva!
Yes, I know that the political term now
is Black –
(*gesticulating and pointing at herself*)
– but she is no more black
than my red-nosed, blue-veined,
blotchy pink skin is white.

Well, Reva, my (*with emphasis*) friend
feels the same about the lifts.
So we share the stairs between us,
arm in arm against the world

*The light fades on NANCY as another spotlight opens
on left corner stage, where REVA is standing on her
balcony, tending her plants and looking thoughtfully
towards the audience.*

REVA: Well, since I had my hip replaced
        it's only my friend
        who could get me to walk those steps ...
        (*speaking directly to the audience*)
        At the hospital
        I can only say that I was frightened.
        You know,
        to have teeth replaced

gives discomfort
but to have hips replaced ...
(*She shakes her head*)
I was in the hospital for three months
– one of the first operations for that,
I'm told –
and Nancy climbed the stairs
to see me everyday.
(*with emphasis*) Everyday!

The spotlight now goes up on NANCY *too, right corner stage. Both characters address each other but look at the audience.*

NANCY: I took the lift once.

REVA: Yes, you took the lift once.
I didn't expect that I'd make it,
But Nancy made me make it.
The hospital got me
so depressed and downhearted.
But Nancy brought herself to me,
sometimes with flowers
– flowers she said she'd borrowed from
the park –
and she'd bring cooked food.
And those nurses!
She used to tell them off
if she see them sashaying past my bed
because them days
they didn't like to see coloured people—

NANCY: (*interrupting*) Black!

REVA: (*smiling, continuing*) —in their hospital.
She even boxed one of the patients

in the bed next to mine!

NANCY: Well ... more of a cuff.
REVA: (*turning round and looking at* NANCY)
It was a box, Nancy.

NANCY: (*to the audience*)
Yeah, well my fist was clenched,
a good right-hander,
a south paw like my husband would have done...
God rest his soul

REVA: Because the patient was complaining
that she didn't want to have a bed next to
mine. (*Chuckles*) Nancy told her
a grave is just as comfortable
as a hospital bed
when your heart is cold

NANCY: I said: warm up a bit! Who'd want a
miserable sod like you up in heaven?
Too right I did!

REVA: I always say that if you can go to sleep
thinking about somebody
and you fall asleep smiling,
God is tucking you in.

NANCY: (*turning to* REVA) Well I love you Reva–
good old-fashioned love,
down to the bone marrow –
and if you needed any good parts left on me
I'd give you a transplant.

REVA: (*to* NANCY) I know you would.

NANCY: (*Raising her voice*) And I know
(*emphasising*) you would ...
and I know people say we're all the same
apart from our colour,
but we're not,
we're all different – and thank Gawd for
that!

REVA: (*looking round, wary of people hearing*)
Sshh!

NANCY: (*Clenching her fist that holds the cloth
and leaning forward towards the audience, over the balcony*) Yes, 'sshh!'
But more important than that ...
it was you who knocked at my door first
when you didn't know me.
You didn't see or hear me for two days
but when I let you in
you nursed me through
the worst winter of my life
of my life
of my whole life.

There is a pause. NANCY *straightens up and re-
laxes.*

Shall I brew a pot of tea, love?

REVA *smiles and nods.*

(*The curtain falls*)

Tip Tap Crack

A young black man
crouches in an unfurnished bedsit.
His floor is carpeted
with twisted empty beer cans
and he rocks
to a tip tap rhythm.

Tip.
Be kind, be courteous
Tap.
It doesn't erase your colour,
just makes it easier to tolerate you.

His long locks
are not tied neatly between his shoulder blades,
or
pushed modestly under his hat.
They bleed upwards
from his mind
and dry quickly.

Tip.
His father said he should cut his locks
and find himself a job
Tap.
Now he's bald-headed and unemployed.

Tip Tap

Tip Tap

This tip tap rhythm
aches in his body,
as he smokes another herbal cigarette.

His probation officer
is too afraid to visit,
always wondering how long he'd take
to crack his tip tap trap

The probation officer
decided to take no chances
and sent the police in
to bring him out.

A police van
is a real small place
to contain all the pressures and frustrations
of his disrespected soul.
On his emotional release,
he was charged
with causing grievous bodily harm
and the destruction of a police van.

He can still hear the judge's long lecture
on his *menace to society*

The young black man
begins weeping,
on realising most of the confusion he has ever
known
has come from
outside of him.

Now he's free.

Tip

He began to use his truth, his strength,
His ability to succeed
Tap

God,what a feeling ...!

Shame/I'm in College Now

Other people's stories
Our stories
Other people's children
Our children

She chased the bus so hard,
she reached the doctor's surgery
before the bus could

Shame

She let the man ride her
with promises out of Satan's diary,
then put reins on her mouth –
nearly broke her neck
Shame

She stayed foolish and believing,
until he ate up the insides of her soul.
She couldn't breathe,
so he gave her his breath
'til she flushed out his child.

Shame

He laughed so hard,
it cracked the innocence of her pupils,
'til she had
tears seeping through her eyes all the time.
The baby couldn't get enough
breast milk, competing
with the lust-fever of the father.

He put her and her breasts
on the street,
to pay the rent for his high.
She thought she could run,
but she had no smiles left
to offer for another's friendship.

And it's so hard to run when you're empty.

He gave her street medicine to keep her instincts
dull
and pollute her desire
and named her 'Evening'.

Shame
She loved him
in all the ways
he cajoled her,
down to performing – freaky tricks
with his friends – in the park
She prayed it would rain!

Yeah,
Shame

But when her baby died
she did not move,
did not – flinch
and all the street medicine
he gave her, she vomited it back
into his hands.
Then
while he groomed her replacement in the next
room ...

The hot July sun
reminded her of a power
stronger than his
Beautiful

That evening she crept out of the house,
past *that* room,
trembling with his freshly-crazed sex
and she chased the bus so hard
she reached the doctor's surgery
before the bus could.

Beautiful

She's in college now,
learning things she should have known
a long time ago
and knowing things
a lifetime won't let her forget.

Other people's stories
Our stories
Other people's children – our children!

Us

Shelter, Food and You

Ugly is not a picture,
It is a state of mind
Crushing grapes is not violence
When you are making wine.

I love you deep and twisted
Like some unsolved crime.
If your family cannot find you
You are in this heart of mine

I love the way you carry
Your deep dark self.
Some people want that glory
Like a trophy
To put upon a shelf
But the very scent of you
is good for my health

All I want is *you, food* and *shelter,*
Shelter, food and *you*
In every room a mirror
To catch me loving you, loving me, loving you,
loving me

People think they know you
But honey, please,
I still ain't met
All your personalities.

If they ever knew you like I know you,
They would call the police

– mood swings,
my dear,
from the kiss of life
to the lash of the seven seas.

People sing river deep, mountain high
But you rock me to the earth's core
And lift me to the sky
My body gets exhausted
But my soul gets up to fly

All I want is *you, food* and *shelter,*
Shelter, food and *you*
We can be each other's river
To bright smiles avenue

People talk about ambition
What is that if your heart is not free?
What is the point to life
Without trips to ecstasy?

Racism, Sexism, Fascism … Ageism
Out there daily – baby – despite that
Let's dare to be all that we can be,
Let love be our landlady.

People say I'm too romantic
Because I do for love
What love does for me.
When I see how they're living
I know I've won the lottery

All I want is *you, food* and *shelter,*
Shelter, food and *you*
Life's a helter-skelter

But God will see us through

You, food, shelter,
Shelter, food and you,
We can be each other's river
To bright smiles avenue
You, food, shelter
Shelter, food and *you*
In every room a mirror
To catch me
                Loving you,
                        Loving me,
                                Loving you, loving me
                        Loving you
                Loving me.

A Baby Doesn't Really Die

A baby doesn't really die
...does it
I heard him breathing out
And in
And out
... and in my sleep
      he was laughing
and my breasts were tingling
adjusting their aim
           from my baby's pretty face
      to his waiting gums

           but he just lay there

breathing in
and I waited
with my milk
      soaking my nightdress
myself breathing in
           and his teddy bear
sat at the end of his cot

with one ear still damp
           from my baby's playful suckling

while my breast hung
abandoned

then I gripped his little nose
and gently pressed my mouth
      against his tiny lips

and massaged his heart

I had
I had to
        breathe out

He didn't want my breath or my milk
When I woke I was soaked in milk
and he twitched
momentarily
in my empty womb.

Bus Stop

One elderly woman
at the bus stop
with her umbrella tucked inside her cardigan,
    and she's waiting
    patiently
for the 276 Hackney Homerton Hospital bus to
come along.

It's mid-afternoon,
the traffic is fair
and once the bus arrives
the journey
    is only 20 minutes there.

It's been ten minutes
but she's not too fussed,
she's waited an hour before
for this particular bus.

The school bell is ringing.
She is soon joined
    by six schoolchildren
playing push and pull.
    She tightens her grip on the umbrella
but remains gracefully cool.

    Five minutes more
her position is safe
but she slides
inches forward
to reaffirm her place

As the queue stretches longer
her heartbeat quickens
as she turns to notice
queue dodgers strategically positioned.

There's one by the shop doorway,
        one by the bin,
                one doing his shoelaces –
                        she'll keep a special eye on him.

One taking overlong checking the bus timetables
        one hip-swinging, gum-chewing, rude girl
                tuned into her personal stereo.

She has to see her dear Rufus.
        The hospital only allows two hours per visit
and today for the first time
        she intended to get
        every minute of it

At last the bus turned the corner
and the queue quietly cheered
then gently surged forward,
but nothing too severe.

Then before the movement
became too ruthless
and the push, shove, spring began,
        she wielded her umbrella
and whiplashed the charge to a peaceful stand.

Nobody moved, everybody stood stock still
        as she boarded the bus,
greeted by a trembling bus conductor.

She said, 'Take me straight to Homerton Hospital
And don't bother to pick up
    Any other passenger.'

The bus arrived quickly
With the lady in good spirits.
She had more time for Rufus than before.
    She said,
        'Darling, remember they damaged your hip
        at the bus stop where we live?
        Well, they won't mess with us any more!'

Flight

When pain prepares to break me,
I know
that I possess
a pair of wings
that can raise me from harm
-Flight

One night
I travelled across the Mediterranean Sea.
It was difficult to find my bearings
on my first journey.

I could never quite keep my balance.
I could not quite feel at a safe height
And I remember the nervousness
of my first
        -Flight

One summer
I travelled to a *promised land*,
at the other side of the galaxy.
I saw Mother Theresa
dancing cheek-to-cheek with Mahatma Gandhi;

Martin Luther King roller-skating,
conversating,
with John Lennon
and Bob Marley.

Swooping and rising,
floating and diving
through blue-black midnights
and yellow-red sunsets.

I learned
how to read the breeze,
hold on to my beliefs
God made our soul a magic carpet
It's a shame really
how characters like Superman
make flying appear so unreal,

By taking to the air
in shiny red boots *and* ...
tights ... *tights.*

Well, to tell you the truth
I tried a pair
and really liked how they feel.
Those snow-capped mountains
can give you such a chill.

My most memorable trips have been to
Rio de Janeiro, Trinidad
and the jazzy blues of New Orleans
I pulsated on the rhythms,
swayed to the beats
that brought to life
my most
elegant of wings.

Flying is something that anyone can do.
Flying is
something that
anyone can do
as long as your soul and mind
are without restriction.

Chart a course to fresh skies.
Rise

Let your spirit feel
total liberation
Of human

            -Flight

'Where do you want to go?'

You Probably Saved My Life

For one kind gesture
I became too scared
and too hungry

Then I became
too unconcerned
to worry
And if our daily bread
is supposed to come from those around us ...
well, the people I know
have never been over-generous.

But your touch
is so tender,
so easy to digest
... you probably saved my life!

Warm Room

There's a warm room
inside my head,
which is heated by the sun.

There are no doors on it
it's where I sit
and watch for her return.

She is an angel,
this lady who last passed.
We wept together
and moved each other,
through the future
to the past.

She left an old diary
on the table,
which I have never read,
because every time
I get through two pages
I remember
How she left.

And her sex refreshed my life:
the heat of summer … with winter's appetite.

She is a soldier…
She is a soldier and a lover
who fought more than she kissed;
her love and fight are badly missed
when our spirits mingled I felt blessed.

Yes.
There's a warm room
inside my head,
which is heated by the sun.

There are no doors on it for privacy.
It's where I sit
And watch for her return.

God Must Be a Woman

And when she smiles
men want to be the reason
Falling over each other
for one sweet moment to be with or without her

And when she cries
men shrug their shoulders
or maybe offer extra kisses
and a few well chosen phrases

Then there's the miscarriage
The stillborn if not the birth
of all the people
Ever
Alive or dead
On earth

And when she bleeds
men have no common behaviour
we cannot comprehend
the depth of the pain
So many ignore her

God must be a woman

Who else could understand
The childish ways of man?

I'm Not a Soldier

You turn your back on God to confront me
You must think that all God's children are easy

I am not a soldier.
Who is born a soldier?
Who is born an enemy?

We fight for many reasons
But if we think about these reasons
Wouldn't it make more sense
To live good and love deep
And let be?
I can drink with you
I can build with you
We can put life on a higher plane of living
or
I can destroy what you build
Deprive you of water
and
In your revenge
We simply exchange
Places in this suffering

In this life there is much music
Many dancers
Without partners
Many feelings
That we do not try

But now I have loaded my gun
Taken off the safety catch
For the brutality
That you bring to my life!

My Quiet Storm

Days like pictures in a gallery,
feelings like colours in my memory
where you've been, what you've done
ain't yet met my quiet storm.

Look at yourself

You turn your back on God
To confront me
You must think all God's children are easy
If so it be?

Bring your ego trip
See if it can outlast the universe of me

After night is day
After day is night
Animal, vegetable, mineral
What is for you is yours
What is for me is mine

The everythingness of good, the emptiness of evil

You want to make your mark on the world
You want to make your mark on me

Don't let it be my blood that you spill
When your blood is as rich and plush
As blue and as lush
As mine could ever be

Find rhythms from your heartbeat
Seasons for your mind

Courage to live and let live
And stop sniffing my behind

After life is death
After death is life
Everything is everything
What is for you is yours
What is for me is mine
The world is a heaven, a hell,
a playground, a ghetto,
everybody needs a friend

Life is of priceless treasures
When you deny me mine
You already deny yourself yours

Look at yourself
                    Move from me!

Days like pictures in a gallery,
feelings like colours in my memory
where you've been, what you've done
ain't yet met my quiet storm.

The Virus
(HIV Positive)

Her eyes
Followed strangers,
Wondering who else beside herself
Had the virus

The sweet moaning sound
Of the saxophone
Mingled with her blood
Her lips quivered
With tears that were
Just below the surface
Lips that I longed to taste

She kept me at bay
With smiles and off-beat desires
Like catching rain between her toes
And kissing friends in the manner of Eskimos
All manner of unnumbered kisses
Were rehearsed in my mind
As she leaned out of reach
One more time

'Talk to me,' I whispered
So she did

'Long days
where I can't reach the end.
Should I give up this time,
before I lose my mind?
Needing, but not knowing
a friend

I would call, but you are so difficult to find.

Do I shout out the pain that I'm feeling,
or simply carry it inside?
Do I ask you for a better meaning
of that which won't let me be satisfied?

So it seems, so it feels.

Lost days
which I may never regain
still wander through me,
still mean a lot to me.
Only watching you
am I able to explain,
the comfort I once knew,
I now know again.

Do I offer you what I cannot find,
or let you find another?
Do I soak our moods with sweet strong wine,
or love you sober and sombre?
So it seems, so it feels.'

I stayed thoughtful
Just inside kissing distance

While her eyes followed strangers
Wondering
Who else beside herself
Had the virus.

Sex is good,
love is better
sex is just a flash,
love is bound to last
through winter summer
                summer winter.

I Ain't All That!
(Private Festival)

It's a quarter past nine
He walks to the window once more
Listening for the click of her heels
Or the slam of her car door.

She said that she'd be there at six
Though he reflected that she'd been late often,
But this time, she had the occasion planned
So it shouldn't be a problem

    The table was set,
    As the clock ticked over
    And sun went down,
    He re-adjusted the chairs,
    Re-rehearsed the lines
    That he'd say once she'd come.

He walks over to the easy chair,
Though he finds it difficult to relax,
Because every time he hears a sound,
His body reacts.

    He bathes his body
    To freshen his mind
    And it's easier to cry in the bath
    The salt-tears mix with the lavender fragrance
    He put in
    To remind him

    Of the July heat
    Of his happiness

He touches his body
With the sensuality
That she taught him

The door knocks
He opens it
Dripping wet but happy
She says,
>'I'll be late more often if that's how you
>greet me!'
>She joins him in the bath
>And hums a melody that he doesn't know,
>But still joins in after a while

They dry each other with kisses
And she whispers
'I ain't all that!'
He whispers back
'You are the spirit in my white rum cocktail
Motown songs that move and chase the blues
from my world
you are,
you are my,
you are, my private festival!'

Streetsong

Ease on by
Don't stop to say hello, goodbye
Find a friend to take you home
I'm not the one

Angry, mad, twisted, blue
Yellow, black, white, red, brown we are
and the beautiful mixture,
of the same blood
under the same star
Some want to be rich
Some just do not want to be poor

And the world goes round and round
Violence speaks
When words fail
Victims treat
Their hearts like a jail
Morning digs deep
Trying to break the spell

And love weeps, within, her street song!

He put a peacock up inside her brain
Made her feel like silk in the ghetto terrain
Showed her off to his friends
and she fluttered like a butterfly,

drawing eyes
from losers, sinners,
survivors and beginners
who took turns to smear her 'innards'
and etch their spite across her fresh young sky.

The child is now carrying a baby
Not knowing which seed came from which daddy
Which seed is HIV
They never rubber-stamped their plans
If sex is good
Then love is great
Sex could never conquer hate
Orgasms burst and babies wake
The midwife wipes her hands

Round and round and round we go
thinking of joy dancing with sorrow
Round and round and round we go

Slow down, it will do no good to run
You cannot outchase the sun
Heat just keeps pouring down
on you, me, him and her
– Forever

We're ignoring God
Remember this is God's back yard
But you
Imitate the devil so damn good
Good love goes to waste

Yellow, black, white, red, brown we are
and the beautiful mixture,
of the same blood
under the same star
Some want to be rich
Some just do not want to be poor

And the world goes round and round
Violence speaks

When words fail

Victims treat
Their hearts like a jail
Morning digs deep
Trying to break the spell

And love weeps,
Love weeps within her!
Love weeps within her street song!

Be Kissed

It don't have to be midnight
for you to want to sleep
The world keeps turning
and your troubles will keep

Curvy women smile out of practice
what's really going on
is covered over by the actress

Below the stars
all human life shimmers
beautifully – yet too many of us are disbelieving

So we create pain
so that we'll know where we've been

And I've told the truth
to escape my condition
only to be ignored by those
who I wanted to listen

So my best conversations
have been with myself
but of course your own mind
can turn against you
without the belief of somebody else

It really doesn't matter
who you think you are

God has more than enough love for you

Be kissed

And know that you are not alone
A morning of happiness
an evening of blueness
Draw open the curtains of your heart's
front room

It don't have to be midnight
for you to unpack your secrets

It's just a shame, sometimes,
that the lover you choose
does not always know
how to show
you what love is

Still, when your vibrations
sense familiar
... *be kissed*

Quiet Power

There is such a thin line
between how I felt
and what I am prepared to do,
to feel that way once more.
For one moment
– one hour

And I cannot sleep,
unless I touch her once more.
To be touched by her once more,
to hold her once more.

The importance of sleep
I can easily ignore,
but not her quiet power ...

And joy arrives without trying,
stays without strain,
eases all pain,
intoxicates my brain;
I've learned to live with magic.

Woman, weave your spell again.

There's no need to brag
Or lock it deep inside
It was as good for me at the same time

It may be a souvenir
In her mind's collection,
But it's my prize possession.
My choice, my passion

There is such a thin line
between how I felt
and what I am prepared to do,
to feel that way once more.
For one moment
– one hour

I cannot sleep unless
I touch her once more.
To ... touch her once more
to hold her once more

The importance of sleep
I can easily ignore,
but not her
quiet power

Purest Water

There are some unscrupulous vagabonds
stealing our sky,
bit by bit,
I can feel it

And all our babies,
are growing up in a skyless world –
no wonder their life is so dismal.

One of them (I don't know which one)
did creep into my yard and
t'ief my TV.
I did love my little portable TV
(even though it could only ever pick up BBC2),
at least you could get a little good weather in there.
Sky and elephants freely roaming
... poor elephants, eh?
Killing them for their teeth

Dentist and I don't have a keen friendship,
but at least, so far ...
they ain't kill me yet.

Why don't we all go to the government
and demand back our sky?
Why did they throw us in the gloomy hole?
I wonder what they done with it?
So much of sky
and I can't get a little piece.

You can't even drink the water
HIV is in it.
Nobody can tell me differently.

I take a bath with my mouth closed.

The purest water you can get is tears.

What happened to the frigging sky?
Where is it?
I bet they sell it.
They selling water, gas,

Well I have
a whole heap of gas ...
and give it away free
to any and everybody
They selling Viagra
Well Leroy say
He can get it cheap down
the market
        – but anyone who could feel like shagging
        when the earth's roof is caving in,
        have far too much erogenous zone for me

Can't even fly a kite
unless it get lost in all that greyness.

Poor elephant, eh, they take 'im teet'
        and take the frigging sky too.

        The purest water
        You can get is tears

        I'm telling you, I'm telling you

        The purest water
        Anyone can get nowadays
        Is tears!

Excuse me while I bawl!

Day

Here comes the day again,
are you awake?

They say that there are seven days to the week.
They name them
and package them
into weeks, months, years and so on.

But there is no such thing
as just one day,
God spare life,
One single day
Done *over and over again.*

With the same sun
and the same rains
splashed into and around us

We build victims and survivors
out of it,
digging graves and building statues.

Here comes the day again,

Are you awake?
And people gravitate
to a kind of hear-tell shimmering light,
taking for granted
their own horizon.

This light can come
from an abandoned spoon,

or an uncut diamond.
We somehow feel

that the day owes us something.
And why not?
After suffering all the
twists and turns,
untruths and dead ends,
should we not feel that the day owes us something?

But who is going to bring it
and why should they!

When they have been
through the same frigging day
themselves
It is better to drink and bathe
from falling rain
than spend a lifetime
seeking a golden tap

all the time
dying of disappointment

subdued by thirst

Here comes the day again

Take your day　　　　　– Take *your* day
　　　　　– Take your day

　　　　It's　your　day.

Slap Dash

At the closed-down hospital
Gangsters roam with drugs to sell
To dreamers who don't dream too well

Amongst him, her, you and I

To shoot stars through the night
To turn wrong into right
To turn sorrow to delight
Digging shallow for a two-minute high.

Burst Bruised Apple

What should I do
this evening
this evening
when the water tank is empty
and my skin is unfresh
like a burst bruised apple?

And I keep trying
to fall into sleep ... trying to
find my way back
to the safety
of last winter's sleep

where I was hugged
by blankets, warm whispers
and kisses ...
        midnight saliva
mingled in my mouth
and over my body

But this evening
what should I do
when your absence
overshadows ...
        my soul

And here I sit by the window
watching

days flick over
nights slip over
dread tip-toes over
my optimism like a sumo wrestler

And you were so lovely
you were
you were, you were, you were
you are
with a smile that God took time over

But this evening what should I do
when the water tank is empty
and my skin is unfresh
like a burst bruised apple?

Gracefully
(for Wayne Howlett)

Every day
My friend
Spends many hours in a wheelchair
– got to rock and roll,
be on the go

I love the way he burns rubber when he's in a hurry
and just
enjoy the whole movement
when he turns
those wheels real slow.

Doctors said
his legs weren't strong enough to carry him
and for a long time
he felt this wasn't fair
when people next door,
people at school,
people on the television
all walked sort of upright in the air.

He said to me
'I know, you
want to ask me how I feel
and how it is
that I don't often wear a frown
but it makes me laugh to know
that people with all this leg power
spend most of their time
looking to sit down!'

We've played snooker
together.
He uses extra cushions
for a little more height at the table
but there are no ramps
for easier access,
in fact it's like that most places we go to

He says,
'Temporary able-bodied people
don't like the idea of wheelchairs
It makes them feel uncomfortable
I suppose they'd prefer me to stay at home
and cause
their lives less trouble.'

He says,
'But this world
belongs as much to me,
what I cannot walk on
I can roll on just as gracefully.'
Every day
my friend
spends many hours in a wheelchair,
wheeling to a stop and spin.
I love the way he burns rubber
but most of all
I love him for being him, so very ...
Gracefully.

Blue
(African Caribbean)

If and I
Notice you
Sky blue, baby blue
African blue

Like a nighthawk
That nobody sees
The city streets blow so cold girl, you can freeze
You are wrapped too tight girl
Relax and *release*
I long to dance with the beast
That you unleash
To conquer me

I'm a dancer
to the bounce of your heartbeat
to the swing of your dress
to the bells of your laughter
to the impact of your kiss

To songs that ain't been sung yet
Love too fired up
To give a damn about hate
I want to *come...*
But ...
I'm prepared to wait
To hold off 'til some mutual date

You can drapes me up girl
Pull and push me round your world
Hold me captive
In the basement of your soul

Don't worry 'bout your neighbours
They are just getting by
I will kiss your very shadow
And leave you free to *fly*

I've got wings to chase you lover
Over and above a' ordinary level
Don't want to catch you
Just want to be available

I want to be a half smile
In your daytime schedule,
Want to be an out-of-season feeling,
Sensimillia in your winter garden,
Sidney Poitier in the heat of the night
On the silver screen – 'They call me Mr ...'

If and I notice you
Like a gospel hymn
The choir swings its hips to

I'm taken by you
You're like a threatening storm
I was born
To stand up to
I'm a boundary line
You are due
To burst through

Calypso, Blues
Rum Punch, Steel Pans
Ice cold beer
If you weren't this for me ... and more
I would not be here

If and I notice you
Like Scottish bagpipes
Playing a Marley tune
That you *cannot* help but dance to

Don't you worry about your neighbours

They are just getting by
I will kiss your very shadow
And leave you free to fly

Sky blue, baby blue
Caribbean blue

The La La Girl and the Bayou Boy

The atmosphere was heavy
His mood was tight
Matilda's son was grieving
Itching for a fight

He sat still
To keep from blowing his mind
But his mother knew he'd blow
In just a matter of time

His girlfriend was a singer
In a reggae band
She was a joy
And he was her greatest fan

They parted as friends
A healthy separation
Well that is what he thought
'til he found she had taken

His Bob Marley collection

Bayou – Bayou, yo, yo, yo

He tried the major radio stations
to ease his mind
Pop, Soul and Rock-'n'-roll
was all that he could find

His father played his music
to ease his son's pain
but the sound of Frank Sinatra
is not quite the same

His mother took him prayer meeting that evening
prepared to shoot the sheriff and the deputy as well
to chase those crazy bald heads from his soul
She told the pastor,
I don't mind gospel
But there's gonna be some roots rock reggae tonight.

Come on son
Get up, get up, stand up for your rights

He raced to the nightclub
Burst through the door
Reached the stage where she was singing
and let out a roar

I trusted you
and you did this to me
you're just like Delilah
you cut the strength from me

She said

It's good to see you've finally come around
After all the good loving that we've done
But ...

We never went out
walking in the rain
or when the stars
did glow

All we ever did
was buy improvements for your stereo
Bob Marley in
morning, noon and night

I just wanted to see

that there was more to life

She sang

La la la la, la la la ... la la, la means I love you

He took her music
mellow and cool
Bob Marley is his hero
but he couldn't be a fool

He sang, La la la la
Bayou yo, yo, yo … Means I love you too

You hold the records
but let me hold on to you!

Midnight's Appetite

All she needed to do was sing
Then everything would be alright
She could stop evil fists flying
In the middle of a fight
She could ruffle the feathers
Of a bird in flight
She could meet midnight's appetite

She filled her church every weekend
They came to see her
But she did not see them
Yet she pulverised their very soul
Toughened their skin to meet the world

She watched the VH1 or MTV
She saw their shiny costumes and slick routines
They said, she could be there
If she compromised
They talked of profit
But she sang for her life

All she wanted to do was sing
Decorate places where lovers wait
Soothe the wounds of old heartaches
Meet with God when day breaks

She worked in a supermarket
Stacking shelves
Her R & B drifted up and down the aisles
Customers stopped and were moved at the same time
They came to buy Branflakes,
And left with wine

She had a lover
But he could not stay
Her need for harmony
Got in the way
Her skin was soft but her need was mean
Her lick flowed from places he had never been.

All she needed to do was sing
Be in the Rainbow Theatre
On a Seven Sisters train
Be intimate with joy, pain
Ride the curves of a deep refrain

All she needed to do was sing
Then everything would be alright
She could stop evil fists flying
In the middle of a fight
Ruffle the feathers of a bird in flight
Meet midnight's appetite

Meet midnight's appetite

Sweet Rain

When you smiled
And disowned me
I could have crumbled
Like a child
And wept

When you looked at me
And started to make excuses
As to why you had to say goodbye

I agreed with you
To hold my self respect

Now a lot of time has gone by
A lot of water has gone under the bridge

And you ask me
Why I don't smile so often
Why I'm not so optimistic
About the things you mention

Well sweet rain
Washes the streets and freshens the air
But somehow
        Manages
To miss your arrogance
By a mile or more

Syrup Kisses

I was a vexed and troubled man
until she gave me Syrup Kisses.
She made a smile out of my whole body
until all you could see was teeth

She was all the ways of summer.
My heart felt stung by a swarm of bees.
When she finished with my sugar
she lowered me gently to my knees

Syrup kisses
should be put on prescription:
on the hour, every hour
would ease the trauma
of most any condition

She had one or two admirers
from old-time relationships.
Sat outside dejected in their cars,
still addicted to her lips.

I said,
'You are an amazing woman but they seem like
broken men!'
She said,
'I gave them what I had but had to leave them
with what they left me – *nothing*!'
She said,
'Love is very simple
what you have you share
how far can any love go
with sweet promises – but the cupboard's bare?'

It's true
Syrup kisses so full of nourishment and
protein
I could pass for vegetarian

Men talk in bitter voices
About what love has done to them
They say:
'Watch how that syrup turns to vinegar
once it skylarks with your brain.'

When I told her this
She said:
'You cannot live your life for other people
and they cannot live their life for you
why follow them to winter
when you've got your own journey to do?'

She went on to say,
'What's the problem, lover?
Have you been so beaten up by time?
I thought you had the apparatus
to turn my syrup into wine.'

She had me cooled by nature,
yet so hot my body heat
could have boiled rice.

Syrup Kisses make my senses smile
and pick my spirit up
A little bit of sugar is good for everybody
but one don't have to go to the corner shop.

Milkshakes and Swimming Pools

She cradles her daughter
Close to her
Offering comfort from
Her empty breasts

She gently shifts and shields
Her daughter
Away from the circling sun
While flies feed haphazardly
From their weeping bodies

Prayers are murmured ceaselessly
She hears them and echoes them
Between wailing and death

As they huddle
Close to an empty well

Not so close
But not so far away
Indifferent souls
Are playing with mobiles and remote controls

While their children splash
In *milkshakes and swimming pools*

Peacock

He put a peacock
Up inside her brain
Made her feel like silk
In the ghetto terrain
Showed her off to his friends

And she fluttered like a butterfly

Drawing eyes
From losers, sinners, survivors and beginners
Who took turns
To smear her innards
And etch their spite across her fresh young sky.

Violently Tender
(A Song Like You)

A private hurricane
in a sparsely-lit room
where my unheld body
meets the gloom
– where is my friend
in this population boom?
Where is the sun
in this long afternoon?

A song like you
Is not guilty
But it feels like a traitor
Gripping me
With the primal motions
Of a forest fire
Your truth to my bare bones
Is violently tender

I don't want to hear you
But I hear you
I don't want to hear you
But I hear you

I want to take you in
move you in
Breathe you in

Through my nose
My woes
My skin

Hold my heartbeat
Make it wait
Flood the corners of my heart
With your breath
Wear your heat
Like dripping sweat

Breathe you in

Out
In
A private hurricane
In a sparsely-lit room
Where my un-held body
Meets the gloom

Where is my friend
In this population boom?
Where is the sun
In this long afternoon?
Violently tender!

I do not want to hear you
But I hear you
I do not want to hear you
But I hear you

There is no season
Like the one you bring
My indian summer
My Eskimo spring

A song like you *enraptures* my life!

Making Friends With Pain

I'm a black individual
A *sick* man
In a *sick* world
Afflicted
By the afflicted
Since a baby and a child

We are all contaminated
And the world
Spins around the same
Some holding on
Some letting go
Some making friends with *pain*

How much steam
Do you have?
How free do you want to get?
On how many roads must you travel,
How much mystique
must you unravel
before you accept
that you are in it – of it?

Telling children
Foolish nursery rhymes
Not knocking old folks' doors
to check if they are well
Watching them chop down trees
Pollute the seas

While you try to fit your life
inside a ten-second TV commercial

I am a black individual
A *sick* man
In a *sick* world
Afflicted
By the afflicted
Since a baby and a child

Meet Me Anywhere

Meet me,
> Anywhere, anywhere
> anywhere

Where you head-butt the ball so hard
the goalie stands no chance
where you ride the bicycle so well
you can let go the use of your hands

Where your grandmother piles your plate so high
it's as if it is her stomach she's filling
where your mother chases you round the front
room
to rub cocoa butter on your dry skin

> Meet me anywhere

The sky wants you under it
With secrets for you to find
God will tickle you even as you sleep
That's why some days you wake up smiling

But even in a hurricane
You can...

> Whisper, whistle, pull, push,
> shout, cry, smile, laugh

I'll find you
and I'll meet you anywhere

Mookie, Boogaloo, Shalamar
(My Children)

It is as if
tears that rolled around the sun
flushed through my heart
and burst through my eyes
at your first breath.

And the feel of your tiny hands
wrapped around one of my fingers
has made more a man of me
than I could ever make of myself.

It is as if
smiles that were smuggled out of pain
came by to give you dimples

and seeing you
at your mother's breast
makes me search my soul
for all that I can give you

      And I will meet you anywhere
      give you my everything

Anywhere

Midwife

The child is now carrying a baby
Not knowing which seed
Came from which daddy
Which seed is HIV
They never rubber-stamped their plans
If sex is good
        Then love is great
Sex could never conquer hate
Orgasms burst and babies wake

The midwife wipes her hands.

Not Even An Ouch!

Life can be so wretched
It can seem like one is
Struggling – drifting
In a sea
Of razor blades

Until all one can do is shout

But somehow
At a different time
In the same conditions
There is not even an ouch!

God Is, God Has

It doesn't have to be midnight,
for you to want to sleep,
the world keeps on turning
and your troubles, they will keep.

Curvy women smile out of practice
What's really going on
Is covered over by the actress

Below the stars
all human life shimmers – beautifully,
but too many of us are disbelieving,
                    preferring
the cool *friendship* of pain
to the sassy adventure
of chasing the dream.

I have told the truth
to escape this condition,
only to be ignored by those
who I really wanted to listen.

So my best conversations
have been with myself,
but your own mind
will turn against you
without the belief of someone else

                AND it really doesn't matter
                who you think you are,

God is a Sweet and Almighty
        Almighty and Sweet *Lover*

Dress yourself in splendour,
be wooed in places of wonder,
    never miss the setting sun.

    Mornings of happiness
    Evenings of blueness

Draw open the curtains to your hearts front room

Because it doesn't have to be midnight
for you to
    unpack your secrets.
It's just a shame sometimes
that the lover you choose
doesn't
    always
        know
            how to show you what love is!

Still God has more than enough love for you
let your soul mate
find you through your smile so deep
it caresses
the senses
like Pina Colada

Believe and let love be yours,
believe and cut no corners.

Spice up your gravy,
Let the music reach your soul,
the devil will always try to claim you,
but you will always be God's child.

Believe and sing hallelujahs

Because it really doesn't matter
Who you think you are

God is a Sweet and Almighty
                  Almighty and Sweet Lover

Margaret Thatcher and her African Lover

I first met her
in Yorkshire
near the coal mines;
'twas love at first glance.

To hear her beautiful authoritative
vocal chords
put my heart
into a dance

She said,
'You remember when you
were under the British Empire
and Britain was truly great!'

She said
'I'm going to take the power
away from the unions
and squeeze their balls until they break!'

In an effort
to demonstrate her point,
she gruffly grabbed my testicles

(What a grip the Iron Lady has!)

'Okay Maggie!' I squealed

We went off to an African restaurant
like two moonstruck teenagers
in a candlelit corner,
surreptitiously

eating our food from each other's fingers
While we gently swayed
to sensual African rhythms

I reminded Maggie
that African peppers
are stronger than her usual ones.
Caught up in the *amour* of the moment,
she ignored me
and developed a delicate but rousing case of the runs

So off to the hospital we went
but when we reached there,
to the back of the queue we were sent.

Then slyly creeping
and sneaking
Maggie persisted, despite everyone's concern,
but the head nurse bellowed to Maggie:
'To the back and take no U-turn!'

This expression had a very big impression
on Maggie
and on her rise through power
she closed down many hospitals mercilessly.

She changed, so we parted,
but I believe it was not all Maggie's doing
they used her to gain power
then wanted to send her back to greengrocering

D'you know, to spite me
she tightened up on the immigration bill?
She said:

'If this *English Rose* cannot have your sunshine
Then no African Azalea will.'

Maggie, Maggie, Maggie,
Out, out, out
they wanted you.
I am a mere man, what could I do?
I wrote to Nelson Mandela
For his point of view.
He wrote back:

'Dear boy, I think you have bitten off,
more than you can chew!'

We will meet again,
don't know where, don't know when
But I know we'll meet again
some sunny day.

Woman Go, Come Bring!

Woman go, come bring
Your basket of ironing
Let me put a sweet crease in your linen

Woman, let me go come light a candle
For our shadows to dance up on the ceiling

With your breath like peppermint and honey
You are so mellow and contrary

And woman you are so strong when you're ready
You are the only one that can lift up my soul.
Should I die tonight
Of feeling so satisfied
It's pure smiles I'm leaving in this world

And you're raw when you're ready,
but you make me feel so fulfilled.
I had a sweet girlfriend before,
but you are so much more.
I'd rather be scorched by your fire,
Than sniff her daffodil

Woman go, come bring
Your blues and soul
Don't leave it home to spoil

Woman go, come bring
Your blues and soul
You know it's wrong to cage your animal

I feel that you feel that what I feel
Is absurd

Flights of fancy
In a pessimistic world
But if I am, are you not just a little stirred?

Woman go, come bring
Your blues and soul
Let it wrestle me to the ground

Woman, let me go come bring my sunset
To your rain falling down

Woman go, come bring your ...

                              You!

Think and Tell me Something

I don't like to take things for granted
When they took so long to arrive
And though it's easy for you to please me
I like to know
That you too are satisfied

Think and tell me something
Because I've been thinking
Of walking away

I won't challenge what you stand for
But your touch
Has become stale
And if we've both nothing
Left to offer
Wouldn't it make sense
For us to reach out of our empty world

Think and tell me something
Because I've been thinking
Of walking away

We use the word *forever*
Much too easily
And I don't know
If our sorrow
Will find itself free

You better
Think and tell me something
Because I've been thinking
Of walking away

God's Back Yard

Slow down
      It'll do no good to run
            You cannot outchase the sun

            Heat just keeps pouring down
            On you, me, him, her ... forever

We're ignoring God
Remember
This is God's back yard

            But you imitate the devil
            So damn good
            His shadow is on your face.

Sergeant Sweet Potato

So this is the big city, eh? Can't even catch a
sign of the stars!
When last did anyone see any stars?
If you're lucky you might catch a shot of bird-
shit in your eyes, but stars ...? Tcha!

Bob Marley and John Lennon, they is my stars,

They didn't like John Lennon because he was
with an Asian woman (*pause*) Yoko Ono

But she make him happy. I wish someone would
make me happy in this skyless, starless city
(*He dances in a sideways shuffle*)

Come on, let's talk
What're you doin',
dreamin',
what you dreamin' about?
Sumthin you can't get up and make happen?
Get up, get up and live life, man
ain't that what it's for...?

I make my own orange juice with lemons
to give it more bite.

The purest water you can get
is tears

(*pause*)

God been cryin' for years

Look how them politicians
closed down all the hospitals,
with only little clinics open up –
one for you ears, nose and throat,
one for your foot,
one for your eye

What happen if your foot and your eye
hurt you at the same time?
You be limpin' and crashin' into everything
and never find no bloody place.

God's been cryin' for years.
I'm tellin' you.
I'm tellin' you.

Dip Your Soul

Dip your soul
In sunny waters
Mend the shovel
Of your fathers
Weed the garden
Of your mothers

Feel the pulse of where
You once were

Bring the music
From the shadows
Let God
Flow through your empty channels
Free your spirit
From the gallows
And let your seasons stir

*'For me, performance poetry means
capturing compassionate, sensual, angry
and funny moments, then letting
them have their way on stage.'*

Photograph by
Juliet Garret